Santa Returns

By

Glyn Davies

Copyright © 2023 by Glyn Davies

All rights reserved, no part of this book may be used or reproduced in any form whatsoever without written permission except in the case of brief quotations in critical articles or reviews

This book is a work of fiction. No names characters, businesses, organisations, places, events, and incidents either are the product of the authors imagination or are used fictitiously. any resemblance to actual persons, living or dead, events, or locales is entirely coincidental

Printed in the UK

For mor information, contact:

glyngregdavies@gmail.com

www.glyndaviesbooks.com

Book design by Glyn Davies

Cover Artwork by Robin Davies

IBSN- paperback 9798862894165

IBSN- Kindle

IBSN- Audible

Sandra Claus stood back and looked round the room she had just cleaned and polished. She felt a great deal of pride in her home and took a lot of time making it look its best.

The house was a large log cabin with moss growing on the roof, set in a clearing in the woods with other buildings scattered around.

At the front was a long open porch with a swing seat and several wooden chairs with wide open steps leading down to the large clearing at the front.

Back in the room, Sandra put some more logs on the open fire and adjusted some of the ornaments on top of the heavy wooden mantle over the fireplace. At the end of the room was a large open staircase leading up to a galleried landing, leading off to the bedrooms and bathroom.

Either side of the staircase on the ground floor was the large kitchen to the right, with the downstairs toilet to the left.

Sandra pulled the two large armchairs round a little closer to the fire. She knew it was going to be cold tonight so wanted the room nice and warm for when he got home. Putting the television remote on the table next to his chair, she had one last check round the room, to make sure everything was perfect.

Sandra stood on the open porch wearing a large thick woollen coat, her long white hair falling down over her collar. Looking to the south, she glanced across to the workshop where the lights were shining out onto the yard, the sounds of muffled voices and of people working came from inside.

Her attention suddenly turned back to the south; a sound of approaching voices could be heard in the distance and was getting louder.

She looked harder through the falling snow to see to see Rudolph's nose shinning like a beacon. "Oh dear," she said to herself, "I'd better get the nose cream ready again"

With that, all the reindeer came hurtling into view as they excitedly approached the cabin.

"Wah Ho lads, slow down we're nearly home."

"Thank heavens for that!" shouted Blitzson, "The smell is getting intense."

The sleigh swooped down and came to a halt at the front of the cabin.

Cupid nodded his antlers and all the reins disappeared releasing the reindeer from the sleigh.

"At last, some fresh air," said Blitzson, "I think I'll sleep outside tonight till those mince pies have worn off."

"Well, I ate the last one four hours ago, so I should be better by now."

BRUMP! "Oo pardon me, perhaps not," said Donner.

"We are going to need the extractor fan going full blast tonight", said Cupid.

Santa had walked up to the steps of the cabin, where Sandra was rubbing cream on Rudolph's nose.

She looked at Santa, "You need to slow down, you're not 200 years old anymore, look at the state of his nose again," said Sandra.

"Yes dear," said Santa, who promptly sneezed and slipped over in front of the steps.

"Did you come back through Norway again? You've caught a cold again, haven't you? I told you to tuck your vest in," said Sandra.

"Well, the lads like to come back that way, it makes them laugh when Donna farts, because it echoes through the fjords," said Santa.

"It doesn't make me laugh," shouted Blitzson "I'm taking a cork next year."

Santa walked up the steps to the front porch. "And wipe your feet!" shouted Sandra. "Yes dear," he replied.

He walked into the cabin and took his coat off, then hung it on the coat stand by the front door.

He turned and looked at the floor in horror, he had spilt stardust from his coat onto the floor as he walked in. He quickly looked outside to see if Sandra had spotted it.

She hadn't, so he lifted the doormat and brushed it underneath, then quickly walked away before she noticed.

Sandra came inside and went into the kitchen to prepare a cold remedy drink for Santa.

Santa sat in his chair and pulled it a bit closer to the fire.

He reached out with the remote to put his favourite cowboy channel on the television.

"I've been looking forward to this ever since we left Norway. It's the 'Big Blast at Red Rock' tonight," said Santa.

"Oh Dear, it's been lovely and quiet while you've been away," said Sandra.

She gave him a glass of Old Uncle Silas's cold remedy to drink. Santa took the glass and put it to his lips, then sneezed loudly and sprayed the contents all over the beautifully polished fireplace.

He looked straight ahead not daring to look at Sandra.

Outside two passing polar bears heard a loud shout of, "AAAAAAAH," coming from inside the cabin.

"He's back," one of them said to the other.

Inside, Santa sat like a statue as Sandra quickly cleaned and polished the fireplace again.

"Sit there and don't move," said Sandra.

Santa pointed the remote at the television and pressed the On button.

The television came on, but the screen was blank with no picture,

Santa frantically pressed the remote button again a second then third time, but still no picture.

He sprang up from his chair and ran to the front door.

He skidded on the mat hiding the stardust, flew up into the air kicking the mat up in the air as well, then fell backwards banging his head on the floor before the mat came down on top of him, covering him with the dirty stardust. He quickly picked himself up, grabbed the mat, opened the front door, and shook it outside before Sandra realised what he had done.

Rubbing his head, he shouted over to one of the elves who was packing away the sleigh.

"Billy, can you go up on the roof and check the aerial? I've lost the signal", said Santa.

"What at my age? I'm not going up there. Ask Willy, he's only a 157," said Billy. "Don't be silly Billy, I can't ask Willy, he's off cutting logs with Nilly", said Santa.

He looked round panicking because his programme was about to start.

"Oh dear, where's Eric? Ned, can you go up and see what's wrong?".

Ned, who was also an elf and only 156, climbed up onto the roof to look at the aerial, which had fallen from the chimney.

"It's broken into two pieces, even I can't repair it, you will have to get Ian the electrician to come out and replace it," shouted Ned.

"Oh Bum." said Santa. "Blitzson, can you fly up and see if you can help."

"Anything to get away from Donna, I need some fresh air," said Blitzson.

Blitzson flew up onto the roof and looked at the aerial.

"No, it's ca-put, it's no good, it's broken, it's finished," said Blitzson.

"Yes, I think they get the picture", said Ned.

"No, that's the problem, I haven't got a picture," said Santa.

"Right, I've got an idea. Go back inside and tell me when you can see something on the television", said Ned.

Santa looked through the window, "Yes I can see something on the telly!" shouted Santa.

"Great, what can you see?" shouted Ned.

"I can see a framed picture of Sandra's Old Uncle Silas standing on top of it", shouted Santa.

All the reindeer were gathered out the front. Cupid shook his head. "Oh no, I can't watch this, I'm off for a lie down, I'm getting one of my headaches," said Cupid.

Sandra dragged Santa back inside before he caused more confusion. Suddenly there was a shout from inside the cabin.

"It's on, hold it there!" shouted Santa

Sandra came rushing out to see Blitzson standing on the roof with the television aerial lead pushed up his bottom and Ned was twisting and turning his antlers to get a television signal.

"What are you doing with Blitzson?" said a shocked Sandra.

"I tried using Donna, but he kept blowing the aerial lead out", said Ned.

All the other reindeer had run off in case Ned called them to help.

Sandra stood looking at Ned for a few seconds then decided to go back inside and not get involved with anything to do with the antics on the roof. She called Eric to ask him to ring Blomforts the electricians and ask them to send an electrician to put up a new TV ariel.

Santa kept dashing from the television to the widow to shout instructions up to Ned as he continued to twist and turn Blitzon's antlers, in an attempt to get a good picture on the TV. Suddenly there was a shout from Santa, "Hold it there, that's perfect don't move ".

Santa quickly went and sat down to watch his programme. He poked the fire then put another log on before settling into his chair.

Pointing the remote at the TV he switched over for the start of his programme.

Sandra looked out the window up to the sky, "It's looking a bit black over to the west, I think there's a storm coming, better close the shutters". Santa didn't reply. He was engrossed in the TV show that had started. She looked across to see he had not heard a word she had said so went around and shut them herself.

Ned looked at the approaching dark clouds, then looked at Blitzson. "Right don't move for the next hour, I don't think the storm will get here for another hour and a half, his programme will be over before then, I will give you a shout when it's finished so you can come down", said Ned.

"Oh, good perhaps the air will have cleared in the stables by then, otherwise Donna will be sleeping in the hay barn by himself.

Thank heavens we won't see another mince pie till next year", said Blitzson.

Ned jumped down from the roof, then went to find Eric to see if he had arranged for a new aerial to be fitted.

Santa sat glued to the television screen. He had been talking about this episode to everybody for the past week. It was going to be the climax of the series as cowboys blasted away some rocks to see if they had discovered more gold. Sandra went round the room again tidying the mess Santa had made when he came in. She was happy to see him back but glad he was in one place for the next hour, as she thought that he couldn't possibly make any more mess whilst sat in front of the television. Oh, how wrong she was.

Ned caught up with Eric to see if he had rung Blomforts. "I had to go and repair the extractor fan in the stables.

Donna was stinking the place out, they were threatening to make him sleep in the hay barn, so I asked Olaf to ring Blomforts", said Eric.

"Oh dear, are you sure he understood because, apart from being half deaf, he's half daft as well", said Ned. "No, no he assured me he'd sorted it, and someone would be round soon", said Eric, starting to wish he had done it himself. "Well, the last time I asked him to go and get me a blanket he came back with a black kite", said Ned.

Santa was now well into the episode of 'Big Blast at Red Rock'. Carl Swagger, the main character, had prepared the mine ready to place the dynamite. All the other cowboys had run out of the mine, so Carl lit the fuse then made a dash for the entrance to find a place to take cover from the blast but, just as the fuse reached the dynamite on the TV screen. Up on the roof a flash of lightning hit Blitzon's antlers. Blitzon lit up like a shooting star, as the lightning shot through his body and down the television aerial lead, which Ned had pushed into his bottom. The lightning shot down the aerial lead into the television which exploded as it blasted itself off the wall, hitting Santa on the head and knocking him out of his chair.

Sandra rushed into the room to see Santa lying on the floor surrounded by bits of what was left of the television. She looked around to see a large black patch on the wall where the television had been with one of her most loved table lamps black and smouldering from the blast.

"What on earth happened?", shouted Sandra, as Santa started to pick himself up off the floor rubbing his head.

"Wow it's these new interactive programmes, they're so realistic", said Santa feeling a little dazed.

"Interactive?", shouted Sandra,

"Look at the state of my lounge! The wallpaper's ruined, my best lampshade is burnt to a crisp and–". But before she could say any more there was a knock at the door. Santa saw his opportunity and quickly ran to the door to open it. He looked out onto the porch to see a black reindeer standing shaking, looking at him. Santa leaned forward to try to understand what the reindeer was saying to him. "What, no we haven't got anyone called Ruth. What? You're Ruth? Well nice to meet you Ruth, what can we do for you?".

At this point, Sandra appeared behind Santa at the door. "Oh my word, it's Blitzson. What happened to you?". Blitzon, who was starting to recover, managed to say he had been hit by lightning and got blown off the roof. "Good heavens", said Sandra.

She turned to Santa, who was slowly stepping backwards to try to escape from the situation.

"Is this anything to do with you? It is, isn't it?". "Err no dear", said Santa very unconvincingly.

Sandra told Blitzon to come inside then turned back to Santa. "Go and call the doctor", said Sandra, "Doctor who?" asked Santa. "Not Doctor Who. No", said Sandra. "Who then?", asked Santa. "Not Who. No". Santa paused and looked at Sandra who was getting quite agitated as she attended to Blitzon who was a little crispy as well as black.

Santa took a deep breath "If you keep saying no to who, who am I supposed to ring?". "NO!", shouted Sandra.

"So you don't want me to ring a doctor", said Santa who by now was totally confused.

Just then Eric walked in to see how Blitzon was. Sandra turned to him and said, "Can you call Doctor No?".

"Yes of course straight away".

Santa looked at Eric. "What?", exclaimed Santa.

"Doctor No, you know, No", said Eric. "Don't you start", said Santa. "Doctor NO", said Eric loudly "Doctor Nosinfinkldonk, but everyone calls him Doctor No for short."

Santa stood for a few seconds trying to compute the conversation that he had just witnessed. He then suddenly realised that he had missed the end of his TV programme. "THE SHOW!", he shouted, "I've missed the end of the episode. Did Carl make it out in time?

Did they find gold? I'll never know".

He rushed over to what was left of the television, slipped on a broken piece of the casing then quickly staggered forwards skidding on the door mat.

 He went flying backwards sending the doormat into the air for a second time before crashing onto the lounge floor, banging his head yet again, with the doormat falling on top of him covering him with all the dirty stardust he had brushed underneath earlier.

He lay there for a few seconds before the stardust made him sneeze, "Ah, Ah, Ah", went Santa as he breathed in all the remaining dirty stardust, then with an almighty "CHOO!", he blew the doormat off him and across the room, sending more stardust up into the air filling the room with a fine layer of dust.

He lay there contemplating what kind of response he was about to witness from Sandra. In less than an hour he had transformed Sandra's beautifully presented room into a battle ground. He didn't have to wait long.

"WHAT HAVE YOU DONE?", shouted Sandra, "Look at the state of my beautiful room, it took me all day yesterday to get it looking nice."

"It's OK dear I can make it right".

"NO don't do anything, do nothing, not a thing, don't you dare try and put it right". Sandra's protestations fell on deaf ears as Santa closed his eyes and thought the magic word to make things back to normal, there was a faint jingling sound in the room. Sandra looked at Santa who was now sitting up with a look of impending doom as he realised that his magic word had not worked,

"What have you done?", demanded Sandra.

"Nothing dear", blurted Santa knowing that something was about to happen but desperately hoping it wouldn't. They both turned their attention to Santa's model Spanish galleon.

It had taken him three years to build, it was four feet long, three feet high and incredibly detailed with everything in working order. The old galleon appeared to be surrounded by a shimmering glow, it slowly lifted off the table it was displayed on, then started floating round the room.

Santa looked at Sandra who was staring angrily at the pirate ship. He closed his eyes to think of the word to make all back to normal.

Unfortunately this only made matters worse as the pirates on board all came to life with the captain waving his cutlass above his head at Santa, as lots of the crew ran up the rigging to let down the sails.

As it continued sailing round the room,

Sandra shouted, "Do something", then looking at Santa, "No, not you".

Blitszon, Eric and Sandra stood looking at each other not quite knowing what to do.

Eric made a lunge for the pirate ship in an attempt to capture it. Unfortunately, the captain saw him approaching and sliced off the top of Eric's hat with his cutlass. Eric leapt back not wanting to lose another part of his hat. Attention then turned to Santa who was trying to stifle a sneeze, "Ah, Ah, Ah", he desperately held his breath to try to contain the sneeze.

This only resulted in building up pressure which led to an even more dramatic "CHOO!". All eyes turned to the pirate ship which was now propelled by the sneeze at top speed across the room towards the Christmas tree, which Sandra had taken a great deal of time and effort to make look magnificent. "Don't worry, I'll stop it", shouted Santa, but this only resulted in all the gun ports on the port side of the pirate opening up, before firing a broadside at the Christmas tree, blasting all the decorations off the top.

Santa stood wide eyed as he surveyed the damage, desperately wondering how to put things right. "I know what to do", said Santa holding a finger up in the air. "Don't do anything", shouted Sandra. By now the pirates had blasted the Christmas tree, shattered two vases, and cut the top off Eric's hat.

The ship was just about to sail round down past the front door when Sandra shouted "Eric, open the front door".

Eric ran to open the door, then as the pirate's ship passed by, Sandra shouted to Blitszon, "Blitszon ram it". Blitszon charged the pirate ship with his antlers and knocked it out into the front porch, where it blasted some more decorations before sailing off towards the elves' workshops.

"AAH CHOO", went Santa, then hearing a "PLOOP", from the corner of the room Santa Sandra and Eric turned to see Blitszon was now a bright yellow colour with fluffy fur and purple antlers.

"I didn't do anything", protested Santa. "Don't even not do anything", demanded Sandra.

"What's happening?" asked Santa, then as he spoke, some ornamental glass ducks took off and flew out the open door.

By now the pirate ship had made its way to the sleigh shed where it had blasted Santa's sleigh full of holes before setting fire to the hay shed. All the elves came running out from the workshop to try to put out the fire. The first to arrive were fought off with a blast of cannon fire which went over their heads and smashed all the windows in the workshop.

Eric, who had chased after the pirate ship, ran to the reindeer stables. "Cupid, come quick, Santa's causing chaos".

"What do you mean?", asked Cupid.

"Well you know how he was last night? He's even worse", blurted Eric.

"Impossible", said Cupid, he paused, then looking at Eric's expression, "No please tell me it's not possible, I can feel my headache getting worse already."

Cupid quickly went round to the elves' workshop where the elves were trying to fight off the pirate ship. Cupid nodded his antlers at it, the ship shuddered then moved forward again. Cupid nodded his antlers once more and the pirate ship stopped then sank to the ground. Immediately the elves surrounded it then threw a large net over it before tying it down. "I don't know what's happening, I've never had this happen before", said Cupid. He turned to Eric,

"Have we got any stardust left?".

"Ooo I don't think so, we used an awful lot of it last night at the Taylors house", said Eric.

"Well take Prancer and Dancer then go to try and collect some. Be as quick as you can", said Cupid.

Sandra got Santa to sit in a chair.

"Don't say anything don't think anything, just don't do anything".

Santa sat staring at the wall as Cupid came into the room. He looked round. "Good heavens what happened?" he asked.

Sandra looked at Santa, "Don't speak", she turned to Cupid, "He brought in some stardust on his coat that fell on the floor then got kicked under the mat, he fell over twice then breathed in a lot of stardust from the floor with the rest of it falling all over the room", said Sandra. Cupid looked at Santa, "Oh dear this is not good, in fact it's quite bad", he spotted Blitzon standing in the corner.

"And what happened to you?", he exclaimed, staring in disbelief at his fuzzy yellow fur and purple antlers.

"I think I look quite dashing; don't you think so?" said Blitzon.

" I think you had better come back with me, said Cupid.

 I will have to go and call Professor Hurtigruten, hopefully he will have an antidote for dirty stardust." He turned to walk away muttering to himself, "Oh dear, oh dear, I hope he's at home".

A few minutes later there was a knock at the door. Sandra had gone into the kitchen to get some cleaning stuff, Santa looked at the kitchen door, then at the front door. There was another knock, so he decided to open it. Olaf stood with another elf who Santa didn't recognise. "This is Ian, the electrician from

Blomforts, he's come to put up another TV aerial", said Olaf.

"Great," said Santa, "come in".

Ian stepped in and Olaf went back to help the other elves, who were still trying put out the fire in the hay barn.

Ian put down his tool bag then turned to Santa, "Could I use your toilet please? Donna gave me a mince pie that has made me feel a little queasy".

"Yes of course it's just back there on the left, Sandra is in the kitchen she will be back in a minute".

Sandra came out the kitchen to see Santa out of his chair. "What are you doing? Who were you talking to?" she said warily.

"It's Ian the electrician, he's come to fit a new ariel".

"Well where is he? I hope you haven't sent him up on the roof, the storm hasn't blown over yet", said Sandra.

Santa was about to explain he was in the toilet but started to sneeze before he could finish the sentence.

"He's in... in... the toil–Choo!", Sandra looked horrified towards the toilet, as there came a rumbling sound followed by an enormous BANG. The toilet door blasted across the room followed by a blackened elf being ejected from the toilet with his trousers around his ankles. As he quickly got to his feet and pulled up his trousers, Sandra looked at Santa who was staring straight at the wall not daring to look back.

She looked at the blackened figure standing by the destroyed toilet door. " Who are you?" she asked.

"I'm Peter", said the elf.

"Well where's Ian?" asked Santa.

"I'm Ian", came the reply.

"So, who's Peter?", demanded a thoroughly confused Sandra.

"I'm Peter", said the elf.

"You just said you're Ian", said Sandra.

"It's Olaf, he didn't hear me properly. When I said I was the electrician, he thought I said Ian. I tried to tell him, but it got too confusing, so I let him think my name was Ian, so I'm Ian, but really Peter".

"Whoo!", shouted Santa, "We can get a new television aerial now."

But before Santa had finished celebrating, noises could be heard coming from the kitchen.

All eyes turned to the back of the room looking in the direction of the kitchen. Sandra then turned to look at Santa who now seemed worried. He wasn't sure if he should be more scared of what was about to happen in the kitchen, or of what Sandra was going to say about it.

His answer came soon enough as the noise of crashing pots and pans, and breaking crockery, with lots of crash, bang, tinkle, clang and smashing sounds filling the kitchen. No one dared to move as the sounds got louder.

Suddenly the kitchen door burst open, and a six-foot-tall octopus crashed through the kitchen door knocking it off its hinges, sending it sliding across the floor towards the fire where it bounced into the fireplace and burst into flames. "Oops", said Santa.

The octopus stopped, looked at Santa then went on a slithery rampage around the room.

Sandra looked furiously at Santa. "Will you stop it, I told you not to say or do or think anything".

"Sorry dear", said Santa. Once again the octopus looked at Santa before snatching the now charred picture of Old Uncle Silas from the top of the fireplace.

"STOP IT", shouted Sandra.

They continued to stand still not daring to move as the octopus ransacked the room,

snatching up in six of its tentacles a cut crystal vase, the television remote, a table lamp, Santa's glasses, some embroidered cushions, and Peter, the elf electrician, before charging past Santa and crashing through a window knocking a huge hole in the wall below it. It rampaged off in the direction of the reindeer stables.

They both stood looking at the hole in the wall for a few seconds before Santa turned to Sandra.

"You always wanted a patio door there", he said, trying to make things seem a little less tragic. Sandra stood and looked at him in disbelief, then grabbed his arm then led him to his chair.

"Sit there," she instructed, "Don't move, don't, don't, just sit there". She rushed to the kitchen, and a loud, "NOOOO, my lovely kitchen" immediately filled the air.

Sandra could be heard franticly clearing and moving things in the kitchen, then she suddenly appeared holding a roll of silver kitchen foil. She rushed back to Santa then quickly wrapped his head in the foil. Santa sat perfectly still not daring to ask what was going on. Sandra finished wrapping his head then smoothed it before tucking it in to secure it in place.

"There, I'm not sure if that will help but it might stop your thoughts from escaping. I'm going to see if Cupid has got hold of Professor Hurtigruten ''. Santa sat looking at the wall desperately trying not to think of anything for fear of what might happen next.

Sandra went to find Cupid. He was in the end stable talking to Eric who had just returned with some stardust. "We could only capture a small amount, we would have had to go to another galaxy to get any more", said Eric.

Cupid looked in the bag, "Oh dear, that's not enough to put everything right".

Sandra looked at Cupid. "Is there enough to sort out the damage out here?" she asked. All the other reindeer were still laughing at Blitzon who was still maintaining that he looked spectacular in yellow.

"You look ridiculous", said Prancer.

"You look like a teddy bear with antlers", said Dancer.

"I think you look cool and dig the crazy antlers maaan", said Comet.

"I think you should get back to normal", said Cupid as he sprinkled some stardust over Blitzon. Blitzon shouted "Noooo!", as he trembled for a few seconds, then with a PLOP, he returned to normal. "Oh poo", said Blitzon, "I thought I looked fantastic".

"No, you looked ridiculous", said Prancer. "Cosmic", said Comet.

"Well I think we can sort the fire in the hay barn to make that back to normal, repair the workshop windows and turn the pirate ship back into a model, but we won't be able to catch the octopus till Professor Hurtigruten gets here," said Cupid gravely.

"What about Peter?" asked Sandra. "Who?" said Cupid. "Peter, no, Ian, the electrician", Sandra replied.

"Oh him, the octopus dropped him as it ran past the hay barn. Ian/Peter ran off, saying get another electrician because he's never coming back. The TV aerial is over there.

Unfortunately, Prancer trampled on it when he got back, so it's broken".

"Well, he hasn't got a television to watch either now so that's not going to be a problem at the moment", said Sandra.

With that Cupid took the small bag of stardust then, flying up into the air, sprinkled the stardust over the hay barn, the workshop, and the pirate ship.

A shimmering light floated down over the barn and the ship as both were returned to normal.

The hay barn was now back full of hay, the workshop windows were back in place and the pirate ship had returned to being a detailed model. The sails were furled up, the gun ports shut and the crew, together with the captain, were back in their place.

Sandra turned to Cupid, "Thank you, you had better keep the pirate ship here till Professor Hurtigruten has made the house back to normal".

"He should be here in the next half hour, he said he had just got to get the Joomakooma back into its pen", said Cupid.

"What's a Joomakooma?" asked Sandra. "I didn't want to ask in case he brought it to show us", said Cupid, "Remember that last thing he brought to show us? It got into the workshop and ate all the pink teddy bears.

The elves were furious, it took them weeks to make another twenty million", Cupid recalled.

Just then Norman, an elderly elf, came running down to Cupid. "Professor Hurtigruten's here", he gasped, "It's OK he's on his own, he hasn't brought that, whatever it was. He's up at the lodge, I need to go and sit down."

Cupid turned to Sandra, "Shall I come with you?" he said.

"Probably best if you stop here, we don't want too many things going on because I don't know what's going to happen", said Sandra.

"Well OK, but I'll wait here in case anything else escapes!" said Cupid.

Sandra walked quickly up to the house to find Professor Hurtigruten rummaging about in the back of his sleigh muttering to himself.

She tapped him on the shoulder. "ARHHH", he turned quickly to see Sandra standing a little startled behind him, "Oh it's you, I thought it might be one of the Essisumps, I've lost one", said the professor, "It's OK though I've left out some mince pies, it can smell one from five miles away, so it will come back for its favourite treat."

Sandra looked at the professor then back to the reindeer shed. She quickly ran back to Cupid.

"Has Donner got any mince pies left?", she asked quickly. "He said he had eaten them all, but gave one to Ian the electrician", Cupid replied. "Well go and search all his hiding places to see if he has any more", said Sandra.

"Why what's happened?" asked Cupid.

"Professor Hurtigruten said he has lost one of his Essisump's and they like mince pies", said Sandra.

"What's an Essisump?" asked Cupid.

"I don't know but I don't want it coming here after the last thing he brought to show us", said Sandra, "Make sure Donna hasn't got a secret stash of old mince pies, you know what he's like".

"Oooh, I don't like the sound of that, whatever it is. I'll go and look now; he'll have to eat them all if he has. It could be a stinkathon tonight if he does.

But it's better than another of Professor's pets rampaging around".

With that Cupid ran off to search the stables. Sandra quickly walked back to the cabin to see another battered old sleigh outside with a polar bear attached to the front.

She quickly realised it belonged to Dr No. "He's inside", said the polar bear.

"Where's Alf, the reindeer?" asked Sandra.

"It's his day off, he's gone snowboarding. He's terrible at it though, last time I had to rescue him from up a tree".

Sandra left the polar bear rambling on about how terrible Alf was at snowboarding, and how he should be fishing down by the ice hole. She went into the cabin to see Santa sat in his chair still with his head covered in kitchen foil. "Well, that didn't work", said Sandra as she surveyed the room.

 A Jamaican steel band were playing on the top landing, in the corner near the toilet was a hook-a-duck stall, except there were real ducks on it splashing around making a terrible mess on the floor – and a palm tree was growing in the opposite corner.

The fireplace was now a rockery, and a giant sloth was hanging from a grapevine growing up the wall and across the ceiling.

Professor Hurtigruten was in deep conversation with Dr No at the dining table. "What do you think you can do to make him better?" asked Sandra.

The professor stopped to look at Santa for a moment, "I think the dirty stardust together with the bang on the head has caused an imbalance in his ability to pronounce the magic words.

I must go and get my case. Dr No is going to give him one of his remedies to stop him from sneezing and making up his own magic words that are not in the book of ancient wizendom".

With that the professor scurried out the room to his sleigh.

"What are you going to give him?" asked Sandra looking at Dr No, who was busy rummaging about in his doctor's bag.

"Ah I have a recipe that I think should work", said the doctor as he mixed several different powders and liquids in a small bowl.

"Have you tried this before?" asked Sandra.

"Err no, but it is listed as a cold remedy used by an old wizard called Slutengulp", said the doctor, who then poured the foul-smelling liquid into a glass for Santa to drink.

Sandra stood by as Santa held his nose before swallowing the mixture. Both the doctor and Sandra stood looking at Santa as he sat in his chair.

There was a slight delay before Santa's eyes widened as he clasped his hands to his stomach.

"Oooh, aah, oh dear" said Santa as he wriggled in his seat, he started to sneeze, "AH, AH, AH CHOOO".

He sneezed with such force he blew himself across the room still in his chair which hit the back wall with a crash, followed by an enormously powerful fart which blasted him out of his chair and onto the floor, banging his head yet again.

Sandra ran over to Santa as he picked himself up off the floor.

"Are you alright?", she asked, quite concerned.

"Yes, yes I'm getting used to it now", said Santa rubbing his head.

Sandra pushed his chair back near the fire, then made him sit down again.

She looked around the room, a little worried about what else might have been added to the mayhem. Surprisingly, although all the other madness was still happening, nothing else seemed to have been added. Her relief was short lived though as a clattering sound could be heard coming from the kitchen. Suddenly all of Sandra's best saucepans came flying through the kitchen door in a line, did a circle of the lounge then flew out through the hole in the wall where the window used to be.

Dr No looked at Sandra, "Well at least we seem to have cured his cold, his nose is no longer red". Sandra glanced at Dr No as she watched her best pans disappear into the woods.

***

Cupid rushed into the reindeer stables, "Have you got anymore mince pies hidden away?", he asked Donna.

"Ooo, err, no", said Donna very unconvincingly.

"That means yes then – where are they?", demanded Cupid.

"Why do you want to know?", asked Donna.

"Because one of Professor Hurtigruten's monster pets is loose and it could be coming here because it loves mince pies", said Cupid sternly.

"Well it's not having any of mine, ooh, that means I've got some doesn't it", said Donna.

"Yes it does – where are they?", demanded Cupid again.

"They're over in the corner under my water bucket", said Donna.

"Well eat them all quick," shouted Cupid. Donna jumped over to his water bucket and moved it out the way. There underneath were three mince pies he was saving for another day.

But as he was eating the last one, the sound of heavy galloping feet could be heard approaching the back of the stables. Suddenly there was an almighty crash as a large bright green fluffy animal smashed through the back of the stable wall. It looked like a hippopotamus but with a long snout, small dumpy horns, two large yellow teeth and bright blue eyes.

It stopped right in front of Donna who was frozen to the spot. The bright green intruder lifted its snout to sniff the air, turning its attention towards Donna.

Donna quickly gulped down the last mince pie as the Essisump's snout came down to Donna's mouth, then suddenly a large yellow slobbery tongue licked all the sugar from around Donna's lips before receding back into the monster's mouth. Donna stood motionless for a few seconds before letting out a huge BRUMP. "Ooh pardon me", said Donna.

The monster stood and looked at Donna for a few seconds, then let out a loud "BLUURRR", before turning and crashing back through the wall of the stables, making a second hole.

Cupid coughed. "How old were those mince pies? That smell is horrible. For Pete's sake go and stick your bum through that hole in the wall", he said.

"I was saving those for another day", Donna complained.

Cupid shouted over to Eric, "Go and see if you can shake any more stardust out of the bag please, we have to repair the holes in the wall now. I don't want that smell wafting back in".

Brump went Donna. Brump pardon, brump pardon, brump oooh I don't feel well Brump.

"You don't feel well? None of us feel very well now! I think I'll sleep in the hay barn tonight", said Dancer.

"Someone get a cork", said Prancer.

***

Dr No and Professor Hurtigruten were deep in conversation about what to do about Santa's bump on the head, when they heard the sound of thundering feet running past the cabin.

They all looked through the hole in the wall the octopus had made, to see the professor's pet Essisump with his snout in the air, heading towards the woods.

"It's Victor", shouted the professor, "He's got the scent of the mince pies, he will be heading back home".

"Don't worry, I'll chase after him and lock him back in his pen", said Dr No. With that he grabbed his bag, then ran out to his sleigh, "Right Malcolm we have to chase after that… that… whatever it is".

"What?" said the polar bear, "I should be sitting at my hole out on the lake fishing, but oh no, Alf wanted to go snowboarding, even though he's terrible at it. I suppose I will be the one to go and rescue him from the bottom of a cliff, or get him down from a tree again, while I have to pull his sleigh all over the place because Santa can't do anything normal like other people, and now I have to chase after one of the professor's pets that's escaped again. Well if we catch up with him on the ice I'm going to kick him in the ice hole".

Dr No wasn't listening, he was busy fastening his bag in place at the back of the sleigh.

"OK Malcolm off we go, quick as you can". Malcolm turned to look at the doctor, "Have you heard a word I've said?". "Sorry, did you say something Malcolm?", said the doctor.

"No nothing", said Malcolm.

"Well off we go then", said the doctor, who was then thrown back into his seat as the polar bear took off at top speed muttering to himself as he pulled the sleigh faster and faster towards the woods.

"I'm just the gofer, I'm going to change my name to Gordon, Gordon the gofer. Yes that's right Gordon the gofer".

The sound of Malcolm complaining was getting fainter as they travelled further into the woods chasing the Essisump back home.

***

Sandra stood looking around the disaster zone that had been her beautiful home. She glanced at Santa, who was sitting in his chair with the silver kitchen foil still wrapped around his head. He sat rigid in place with one eye closed and the other fixed on a nail in the wall where a picture of him on his two hundredth birthday used to hang before the octopus snatched it and crashed through the wall.

She turned to Professor Hurtigruten, "Can you do anything to help, Professor?"

He stood looking at Santa whilst stroking his long white beard, "I think I will have to look into the ancient book of wizendom and hope that we can find a spell to make him normal again", said the professor. "Blimey, have you got a spell that powerful? He's never been normal", said Sandra.

The professor, who was taking the kitchen foil off Santa's head turned to look at Sandra. "What?", he said.

"Sorry it's OK, I'll be happy to just have him back as he was", said Sandra jokingly.

The professor scurried out to his sleigh, then returned a few minutes later carrying a large old leather-bound book. As he walked back into the room, a leather hinged top bag with worn carry handles floated into the room behind him.

The bag followed the professor and sat itself down on the table where he placed the book. The professor carefully took the book cover with two hands and gently opened it onto the table.

Sandra stood quietly, not wanting to disturb the professor's concentration as he slowly turned the pages of the book of wizendom. She looked across to Santa who was still transfixed staring at the wall, then her attention was suddenly averted back to the Professor.

"Aah that might do it", he said. The professor then quickly opened the old leather bag on the table and rummaged inside. He brought out a small square jar containing some sparkling orange powder. He had just placed it onto the table when suddenly a long thin purple tentacle shot out from the bag, grabbed the jar then quickly retreated back into the bag.

The professor turned immediately, "GIVE that back at once!", he shouted. With that he thrust his arm into the bag, whereby he was pulled almost entirely into the bag himself.

The professor's voice could be heard from deep within inside, "Give that back, I've told you about that before". The bag bumped and bounced around the table, with all manner of flashing lights and sounds coming out from inside, "moo, jingle, bang, clatter, woop woop roar, squark, let go".

The noise carried on for several minutes, with the professor managing to pull part of his arm out of the bag before being pulled back in again.

"Will you let go!", shouted the professor, and with that he was suddenly thrown out onto the table as the jar was released.

He placed the jar on the table, then pulled his hat straight.

"Right can someone please pass me the green fairy dust and the elf breath jar", said the professor.

The bag shook and vibrated for a few seconds before the two purple tentacles emerged from the top of the bag, then passed the two jars to the professor, who placed them onto the table next to the jar containing the sparkling orange powder. He turned to Sandra who was standing slightly behind him as she did not want to be too close to whatever was in the professor's bag.

"Do you have a small bowl and a towel please?", asked the professor.

"Yes hopefully I've still got one."

She quickly went into the kitchen, and more crashing and clanging could be heard before she returned with the items the professor had requested. She placed them onto the table then took several steps back, to keep well out of the way.

The professor carefully poured the contents of the elf's breath jar into the bowl then, taking a small silver spoon from his jacket pocket, he carefully measured a small amount of the green and orange powders into the bowl before giving them a gentle stir. He then pulled a chair up to the table before asking Santa to come and sit at the table. Santa carefully rose from his leather chair and walked slowly over to the table, then sat on the chair in front of the professor.

"OK, place both hands on the table face down." Santa did as requested, then the professor took off the kitchen foil cap that Sandra had put onto his head. He placed the bowl containing the elf breath and powders in front of Santa.

"Now lean forward over the bowl."

Santa did as instructed, whilst the professor placed the towel over Santa's head, covering the bowl.

"Now gently breathe in", said the professor.

Santa took a deep breath, there was a slight hesitation before a sudden CHOOO, as Santa threw himself backwards off the chair and onto the floor.

The towel shot into the air then dropped into the professor's bag where a munching sound could be heard followed by a big "BURP". The dust from the bowl was blown up into the air where it floated down covering the room in a light brown dust as the two powders mixed together.

Sandra stood looking at the room. The kitchen door had burnt away on the fire, and the toilet was blackened from the blast.

Snow was now blowing in through the hole in the wall, and the steel band were now really getting on her nerves having been playing 'We Wish You A Merry Christmas' for the past two hours.

She got Santa to his feet, then helped him back to his chair at the table.

The professor was rummaging about in his bag again. Various things kept popping out, to which the professor responded with "No not that or that.

Can someone look in the draw over there? Yes, no not that one. I need the small heavy one. Look in the tall cupboard, yes that's the one can you pass it here please" as he peered into the bag. Several grunts, squelches and woofs came from the bag before a small heavy frying pan was ejected from it, just missing the professor before landing on the table with a thud.

The professor looked back into the bag.

"That just missed me, that's no marshmallows for you tonight".

A groan came out of the bag then it slammed itself shut. The professor carefully placed the frying pan on the table next to Santa, then turned over a few more pages in the book of wizendom, "Ah there it is", he said pointing to some scripture in the book.

Santa looked at the professor and was about to speak when the professor held up his hand,

"No don't speak, I want you to sit very still while I perform this ritual".

"What are you going to do?", asked Sandra, looking very confused.

"No don't speak", said the professor, who then picked up the frying pan and clouted Santa on the side of the head with it.

There was a "clang" as Santa wobbled for a few seconds before sitting upright again.

Pointing to a word in the book, the professor instructed, "Say this word in your head without speaking it".

Santa leaned forward to look at the word the professor was pointing to, then closed his eyes to think of the word. Sandra and the professor looked at Santa in anticipation.

A few seconds later there was a "poof" from the corner of the room.

Standing there looking at the wall was a polar bear. "Malcolm?", said Sandra, "is that you?".

The polar bear turned to look at Sandra, "Not again. I was just about to catch a fish out on the lake, then poof I'm here again.

Do you know how long it's going to take me to walk back there? I should have been there this morning, but I had to come here because its Alf's day off, then it's off to the professor's before I can go fishing, then as soon as I do I'm back here again."

"Well sorry Malcolm, but the professor has been trying to help Santa".

Malcolm wasn't listening as he walked off out through the hole in the wall muttering to himself, "Help? It's me that needs help, 'Malcolm can you help with this? Malcolm can you help with that?'".

The professor reached into his pocket then took out a notepad and pencil. He proceeded to write down several notes together with various calculations as he muttered to himself "Angle, trajectory speed". Sandra looked on wondering what was about to happen next.

Santa sat still in the chair looking straight ahead as the professor put down his notebook, he picked up the frying pan again then paused for a moment before swapping it to his other hand, then with a swift motion he clouted Santa on the other side of his head. Santa wobbled again before falling off his chair onto the floor. Sandra rushed over and grabbed his arm to help him up.

"Are you ok?", she said. "Yes I'm ok, I'm getting used to it now". Sandra helped him back into his chair back at the table.

The professor was busy looking through the book of wizendom again.

He pointed to another word, "Say that word in your head without speaking it out loud".

Santa leaned forward to look at the word the professor pointed to.

There was a faint jingling sound in the corner of the room followed by a dull clunk as the professor hit Santa again with a bit less force.

"Nearly there, just a slight technical adjustment", said the professor turning to Sandra.

"Right, try that word", he said to Santa. Once again Santa did as instructed, a shimmering tinkling sound came from the hole in the wall, when suddenly with a "Ping", the window was restored and the wall beneath was back in place.

Sandra put both hands up to her face, "WOW, you've done it. Does this mean he's cured?".

"Well, we seem to have made him better, I think he will be ok now". "Oh, thank you professor, now I can put everything right. I just have to think the magic word", said Santa.

"NO!", shouted the professor and Sandra together.

The professor opened his bag again, reached inside and took out a small silver globe. He placed it onto his open palm, then gently threw it into the air. The small globe rose into the air, where two small butterfly like wings took it high into the room. It hovered for a few seconds before bursting, covering the room in a sparkling mist that filled the room.

Santa, Sandra, and the professor stood silently as the mist cleared. Sandra gasped as she saw her room back to normal; the toilet was back in place the kitchen door was back on, the television was back on the wall and the pirate ship was back on its stand. The whole room was sparkling clean and polished.

Santa looked at the television on the wall.

"OOOH, does this mean I can watch 'Big Blast at Red Rock' now?", he asked excitedly. He rushed over to his favourite chair and grabbed the remote to put his programme on.

The professor looked around the room. "Well I think my work here is done", he said.

He started to gather his things to place them back in his bag.

"Oh, thank you professor, you've been marvellous, could I keep the frying pan please?".

The professor looked at her a little surprised, "Well yes of course, do you not have a frying pan?".

"Oh yes, I have an excellent one", she glanced across at Santa, "I don't want it for cooking".

About the author

As a child of the 50's I was brought up on the television programmes of Mr Pastry, The Marx Bros, Laurel & Hardy, Charlie Chaplin & many more.
Which is where my love of slapstick and the absurd comes from.

I get the biggest thrill from making people smile. With my writing, I hope to entertain, not just children but anyone who is still a kid inside.

https://www.glyndaviesbooks.com

Acknowledgments

I want to say a special thanks to the people who have assisted me in producing this book

Robin Davies

For his time in creating the front & rear cover artwork

https://www.robindaviesillustration.com

Sarha Khan

For editing my ramblings into a printable book

Graham Mack

For narrating and producing a brilliant audible version

https://www.grahammack.com/

You dear reader

Thank you for buying this book, I hope it makes you smile.

Printed in Great Britain
by Amazon